"What a charming, loving, and imaginative approach to prayer services for young children. Gayle Schreiber has written a wonderful book that begins to teach the young child about God's love in a gentle yet simple way.

"The author imaginatively uses familiar tunes to teach God's love, gentleness, and goodness through song. Young children also learn to respond to God in simple yet direct ways that encourage feelings of unity and gratitude. *Prayer Services for Young Children: 30 Ten Minute Celebrations* is a wonderful approach to prayer and it teaches children in language they can readily understand."

Linda Orber
Co-author of *Dear Jesus, Dear Child*

"Prayer Services for Young Children: 30 Ten Minute Celebrations provides an excellent opportunity for children to become actively involved in the practice of their faith. It exposes them to small doses of Scripture in ways they can enjoy and understand.

"This is a wonderful resource for teachers of young children because it supports the basic preschool religious education themes they are already using. It can also be used effectively by parents of young children, providing many opportunities to share prayerful experiences at home.

Sr. Mary Beatrice Floch, V.S.C.
Principal, Holy Family School

"I found *Prayer Services for Young Children* simple enough for children to understand and clear enough for them to know what is expected of them. Involved primarily with children below the kindergarten level, I am always looking for ways of presenting the idea of God that convey acceptance and love for the child's essential nature. I believe Gayle Schreiber does just that.

"Prayer Services with Young Children will be received with appreciation by all those persons seeking to provide a closer, warmer, living relationship between children and their loving God."

Joan Neth, Program Coordinator
Early Childhood Education
Cuyahoga Community College

"This book offers parents and teachers 30 ten-minute celebrations for children ages 3 to 6. The themes selected by kindergarten teacher and mother of three, Gayle Schreiber, will appeal to both preschool and primary-grade children.

"Each celebration includes an original song, a greeting, a short scripture verse, a group response, a symbol, and a thank you prayer. The drawings of symbols in the book may be copied. These brief, enjoyable, and simple services can be used by teachers in a class setting or by parents in the home."

Pat Durbin
The Catholic Times

"If you have small children but a big desire to pray with them, here's a book to help you bring the two together. A kindergarten teacher, Schreiber has composed 30 brief celebrations of events (e.g., Thanksgiving, Baptism, Christmas, and Valentine's Day), people (families and friends), and things (our senses, colors, and being afraid). Each service includes a song sung to a familiar tune, a scripture verse, and thank you prayer. 'They work very well for me and my kindergarteners,' Schreiber says. 'Mix, match, and adapt them to your own child.'"

Bringing Religion Home Newsletter

"A fine collection of brief prayer celebrations that can be easily understood by children ages 3 to 6. Prayer services focus on themes familiar to young children including: belonging, families, helping, Thanksgiving, saints, Advent, Mary, and Easter."

Bits & Pieces
Newsletter, Winona Diocese

PRAYER SERVICES for YOUNG CHILDREN

30 Ten Minute Celebrations

GAYLE SCHREIBER

TWENTY-THIRD PUBLICATIONS
Mystic, Connecticut 06355

Second printing 1994

Twenty-Third Publications
185 Willow Street
P.O. Box 180
Mystic CT 06355
(203) 536-2611
800-321-0411

© Copyright 1993 Gayle Schreiber. All rights reserved. No part of this publication, with the exception of the line art, may be reproduced in any manner without prior written permission of the publisher. Write to Permissions Editor.

ISBN 0-89622-542-9
Library of Congress Catalog Card Number 92-82674

Dedication

To my husband, Tom, and to our three children:
Matthew, Mary, and Molly—special gifts from God.
And to my mother and father, Angela and Paul Fortlage,
who gave me the gift of life.

Contents

	Introduction	1
1	I Belong to God's Family Theme: Belonging	2
2	I'm a Star Because God Loves Me Theme: I'm a Star	4
3	God Has Given Me a Family to Love Theme: Families	6
4	A Friend Is Someone to Care and Share With Theme: Friends	8
5	I Joined God's Family at My Baptism Theme: God's Family	10
6	God Created a Wonderful World for Us Theme: Creation	12
7	God Put Beautiful Colors in Our World Theme: Colors	14
8	I Go to Church as Part of God's Family Theme: Church	16
9	Prayer Is Listening and Talking to God Theme: Prayer	18
10	We Have Much to Be Thankful For Theme: Thanksgiving	20
11	Advent Is a Time of Waiting Theme: Advent—Week 1	22
12	We Prepare Our Hearts for Christmas Theme: Advent—Week 2	24
13	Christmas Will Soon Be Here Theme: Advent—Week 3	26
14	We Celebrate Jesus' Birthday Theme: Advent—Week 4	28
15	We Experience God's World with Our Five Senses Theme: Five Senses	30

16	We Can Help Others Theme: Being a Helper	32
17	We Can Share With Others Theme: Sharing	34
18	Jesus Is My Special Friend Theme: My Special Friend, Jesus	36
19	God Understands My Feelings Theme: Feelings	38
20	God Is With Me When I'm Afraid Theme: Being Afraid	40
21	We Celebrate Easter Theme: Easter	42
22	Mary Is Our Mother in Heaven Theme: Mary, Our Heavenly Mother	44
23	I Am Growing in God's World Theme: Growing	46
24	St. Valentine Loves Little Children Theme: St. Valentine—February 14	48
25	We Celebrate Mary's Birthday Theme: Birthday of Mary—September 8	50
26	St. Thérèse Was the Little Flower of Jesus Theme: Feast of St. Thérèse—October 1	52
27	I Have a Guardian Angel Theme: Feast of the Guardian Angels—October 2	54
28	St. Francis Loved God's Creatures Theme: Feast of St. Francis—October 4	56
29	St. Patrick Told Us of God's Love Theme: Feast of St. Patrick—March 17	58
30	St. Joseph Was a Loving Father Theme: St. Joseph—March 19	60

PRAYER SERVICES for YOUNG CHILDREN

Introduction

Prayer Services for Young Children: 30 Ten Minute Celebrations is a collection of prayer experiences that center on themes easily understood by children. The celebrations are developmentally appropriate for young children and can be used both at home and in class settings. These are experiential celebrations that allow children to take an active role. Each includes the following:

•**An Original Song.** Each service begins and ends with an original song, sung to a familiar tune. The songs are very easy to learn. With my kindergarten children, I sing the song first and then invite them to sing it with me. We often repeat the song two or three times until the children are comfortable with the words.

•**A Greeting.** This introduces the theme in simple language and sets the tone for the celebration.

•**A Short Verse from Scripture.** These are carefully chosen to introduce children to a loving God. Before proclaiming the verse, I always pick up the Bible reverently. I explain to the children that the Bible is a very special book because God speaks to us through its words. I then read the short verse directly from the Bible, repeating it two or three times. I encourage the children to repeat the words after me.

•**A Group Response.** This explains the Scripture verse and gives children the opportunity to actively participate by verbally responding to God's Word.

•**A Symbol.** These represent the theme of the celebration, and children are invited to color them and cut them out. These symbols make excellent prayer objects for children to hold during the Thank You Prayer. Note: Permission is granted to copy the drawings in this book.

•**Thank You Prayers.** These give children another opportunity to respond verbally to God's goodness and love. In this part of the celebration children are invited to offer spontaneous prayers of thanks.

These simple prayer celebrations have worked very well for me and my kindergartners. I invite all catechists, parents, and teachers of young children to use them often. You need not follow the sequence presented here. Feel free to mix, match, and adapt the celebrations to your own unique child or group. As you experience these simple services, may you and your little ones grow in faith and in deeper awareness of God's great love.

~ 1 ~
I Belong to God's Family

Theme: Belonging

Opening Song: "I Belong to God's Family"
(Tune, "I'm a Little Teapot")

> I'm a special person, happy as can be.
> For God made you and God made me.
> And as I share my happiness with special friends I meet,
> I know we all belong to God's family.

Greeting: I'm so happy to have each one of you here today to help me celebrate God's love for each one of us. We all belong to God's family.

Reading: "…how good it is that we are here!" Matthew 17:4

Response to God's Word
Leader: We all belong to God's family.
Children: Thanks be to God.
Leader: We all belong to a very special group: our family (class).
Children: Thanks be to God.
Leader: God is happy that we are here.
Children: Thanks be to God.
Leader: We are happy that we are here.
Children: Thanks be to God.

Prayer Object: heart *(Give each child a heart to color and cut out.)*

Thank You Prayer
Leader: For this special group we belong to,
Children: Thank you, God.
Leader: We are happy because we belong to God's family.
Children: Thank you, God.
Leader: *(to children)* Do any of you have something special you are thankful for that you would like to share?
Children: Thank you, God. *(Use this response after each child's prayer.)*

Closing Song: "I Belong to God's Family"

~ *I Belong to God's Family* ~

2

I'm a Star Because God Loves Me

Theme: I'm a Star

Opening Song: "I'm a Star"
(Tune, "Are you Sleeping?")

I am special, I am special.
God loves me, God loves me.
God is watching over me.
God will always care for me.
I'm a star, God loves me.

Greeting: We are here to celebrate how special each of us is to God.

Reading: "You are special to me." Isaiah 43:4

Response to God's Word

Leader:	Each of us is very special to God.
Children:	Thanks be to God.
Leader:	Each of us is a star.
Children:	Thanks be to God.
Leader:	Each of us is a star because God loves us.
Children:	Thanks be to God.
Leader:	We are glad that we are special to God.
Children:	Thanks be to God.

Prayer Object: star *(Give each child a star to color and cut out.)*

Thank You Prayer

Leader:	For making us special,
Children:	Thank you, God.
Leader:	We are stars.
Children:	Thank you, God.
Leader:	We're happy to be God's children.
Children:	Thank you, God.
Leader:	*(to children)* Do any of you have something you are thankful for that you would like to share?
Children:	Thank you, God. *(Use this response after each child's prayer.)*

Closing Song: "I'm a Star"

~ *I'm a Star Because God Loves Me* ~

~ 3 ~

God Has Given Me a Family to Love

Theme: Families

Opening Song: "A Family to Love"
          (Tune, "Mary Had a Little Lamb")

> I have a special family,
> Family, family.
> I have a special family,
> A family to love.

Greeting: We are here to celebrate God's gift of a family. God gives us a family to care with, to share with, and to love.

Reading: "Children, obey your parents in the Lord, for that is what is expected of you. Honor your father and mother." Ephesians 6:1–2

Response to God's Word
Leader:	There are many kinds of families.
Children:	Thanks be to God.
Leader:	Each of us has a very special family.
Children:	Thanks be to God.
Leader:	God wants our families to care and share and love.
Children:	Thanks be to God.
Leader:	We will care and share and love with our families.
Children:	Thanks be to God.

Prayer Object: circle of love *(Give each child a circle of love to color and cut out.)*

Thank You Prayer
Leader:	For bringing us together to learn of your gift of families,
Children:	Thank you, God.
Leader:	For our families to love and care and share with,
Children:	Thank you, God.
Leader:	*(to children)* Do any of you have something special you are thankful for that you would like to share?
Children:	Thank you, God. *(Use this response after each child's prayer.)*

Closing Song: "A Family to Love"

~ *God Has Given Me a Family to Love* ~

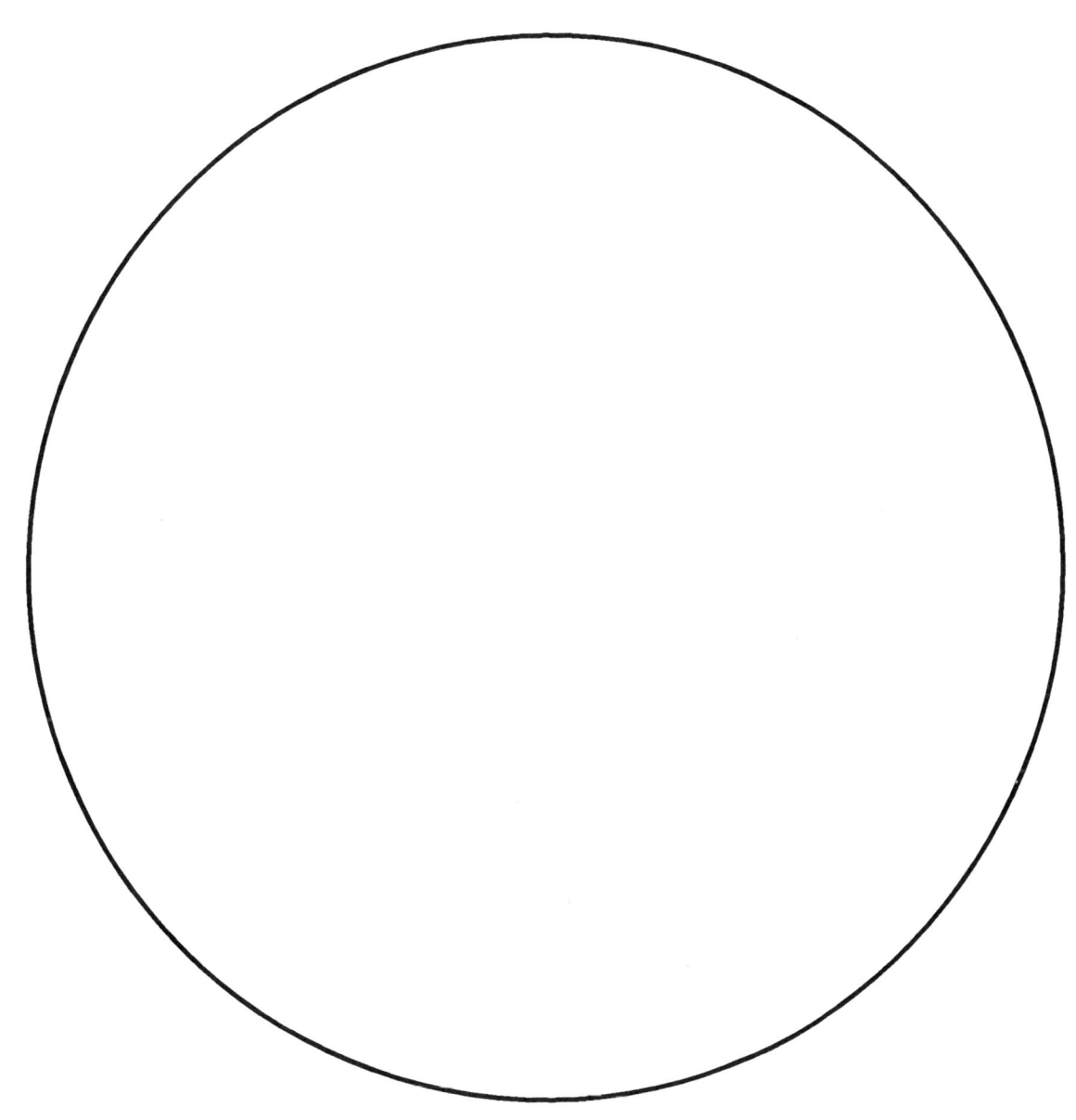

~ 4 ~

A Friend Is Someone to Care and Share With

Theme: Friends

Opening Song: "Friends Are Special"
(Tune, "Are You Sleeping?")

> Friends are special, friends are special.
> They bring joy, they bring joy.
> Somebody to share with,
> Somebody to care with,
> Please be mine. Please be mine.

Greeting: We are here to celebrate how special we are to our friends.

Reading: "I call you friends." John 15:15
"You cannot go wrong with a good friend or neighbor." Sirach 40:23

Response to God's Word
Leader: A friend is somebody to share with.
Children: Thanks be to God.
Leader: A friend is somebody to care with.
Children: Thanks be to God.
Leader: We can bring joy to each other by showing we care with a friendship flower.
Children: Thanks be to God.

Prayer Object: flower (*Give each child a flower to color and cut out and give to a friend.*)

Thank You Prayer
Leader: For giving us friends,
Children: Thank you, God.
Leader: For the joy friends bring,
Children: Thank you, God.
Leader: Help us to care and share with our friends in a way that is pleasing to you.
Children: Thank you, God.
Leader: *(to children)* Do any of you have something special you are thankful for that you would like to share?
Children: Thank you, God. *(Use this response after each child's prayer.)*

Closing Song: "Friends are Special"

~A Friend Is Someone to Care and Share With~

~ 5 ~

I Joined God's Family at My Baptism

Theme: God's Family

Opening Song: "God Loves Me Very Much"
  (Tune, "Farmer in the Dell")

>God loves me very much.
>God loves me very much.
>God will take good care of me.
>God loves me very much.

Greeting: We are here to celebrate how wonderful it is to be a part of God's family. We joined God's family at our baptism.

Reading: "Accept the water...as a gift." Revelation 22:17

Response to God's Word
Leader: At baptism, water is poured over the baby's forehead. Water is important for loving and growing.
Children: Thanks be to God.
Leader: A candle is lighted to remind us of Jesus, the light of the world. The candle gives us warm and happy feelings.
Children: Thanks be to God.
Leader: The baby wears white clothing for this special celebration. White is the color of joy.
Children: Thanks be to God.

Prayer Object: candle *(Give each child a candle to color and cut out.)*

Thank You Prayer
Leader: For making us a part of your wonderful family.
Children: Thank you, God.
Leader: We are special to you. You love us very much.
Children: Thank you, God.
Leader: *(to children)* Do any of you have something special you are thankful for that you would like to share?
Children: Thank you, God. *(Use this response after each child's prayer.)*

Closing Song: "God Loves Me Very Much"

~ *I Joined God's Family at My Baptism* ~

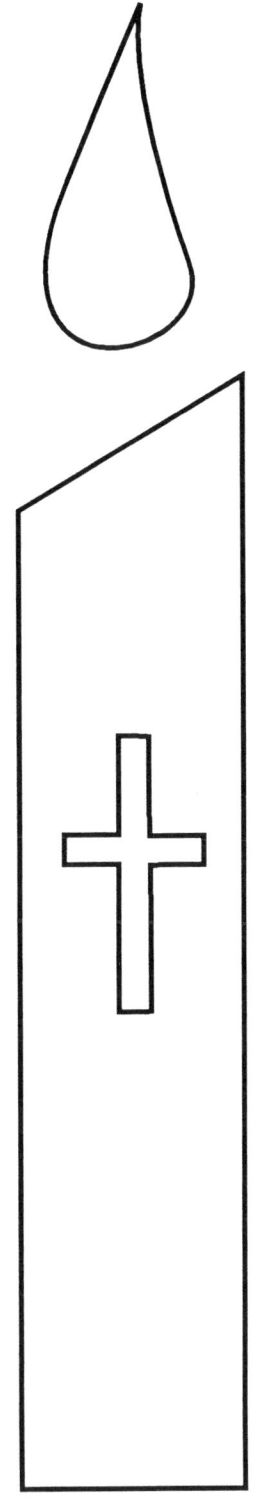

… 6 …

God Created a Wonderful World for Us

Theme: Creation

Opening Song: "Your World Is Wonderful, God"
(Tune, "Farmer in the Dell")

> Your world is wonderful, God.
> Your world is wonderful, God.
> Your world is for us to share and enjoy.
> Your world is wonderful, God.

Greeting: We are here to celebrate God's gift of a beautiful world. God loves us very much. God made a wonderful world for us to live in.

Reading: "God looked at everything God had made and found it very good." Genesis 1:31

Response to God's Word

Leader:	God created a beautiful world for us to use and enjoy. On the first day God created light.
Children:	Thanks be to God.
Leader:	On the second day God created land and water.
Children:	Thanks be to God.
Leader:	On the third day God created plants to grow on the land.
Children:	Thanks be to God.
Leader:	On the fourth day God created the sun, the moon, and the stars.
Children:	Thanks be to God.
Leader:	On the fifth day God created fish to swim and birds to fly.
Children:	Thanks be to God.
Leader:	On the sixth day God created animals and people.
Children:	Thanks be to God.
Leader:	On the seventh day God rested. God made this day holy.
Children:	Thanks be to God.

Prayer Object: sun *(Give each child a sun to color and cut out.)*

Thank You Prayer

Leader:	For this beautiful world you have made for us,
Children:	Thank you, God.
Leader:	We will take care of everything you have made for us.

Children: Thank you, God.
Leader: *(to children)* Do any of you have something special you are thankful for that you would like to share?
Children: Thank you, God. *(Use this response after each child's prayer.)*

Closing Song: "Your World Is Wonderful, God"

~ God Created a Wonderful World for Us ~

~ 7 ~

God Put Beautiful Colors in Our World

Theme: Colors

Opening Song: "Colors"
    (Tune, "Did You Ever See a Lassie?")

> Did you ever see a rainbow, a rainbow, a rainbow?
> Did you ever see a rainbow up high in the sky?
> With bright red and bright blue
> And bright green and bright orange
> Did you ever see a rainbow up high in the sky?

Greeting: We are here to celebrate the beautiful colors in God's world.

Reading: "Great are the works of the Lord." Psalm 111:2
    "God fills your lifetime with good." Psalm 103:5

Response to God's Word
Leader: God has filled our world with beautiful colors.
Children: Thanks be to God.
Leader: For red and blue and yellow,
Children: Thanks be to God.
Leader: For green and purple and orange,
Children: Thanks be to God.
Leader: Our world is full of goodness.
Children: Thanks be to God.

Prayer Object: rainbow *(Give each child a rainbow to color and cut out.)*

Thank You Prayer
Leader: For all of the beautiful colors you have put in our world,
Children: Thank you, God.
Leader: For our favorite colors,
Children: Thank you, God.
Leader: For wonderful rainbows,
Children: Thank you, God.
Leader: *(to children)* Do any of you have something special you are thankful for that you would like to share?
Children: Thank you, God. *(Use this response after each child's prayer.)*

Closing Song: "Colors"

~ God Put Beautiful Colors in Our World ~

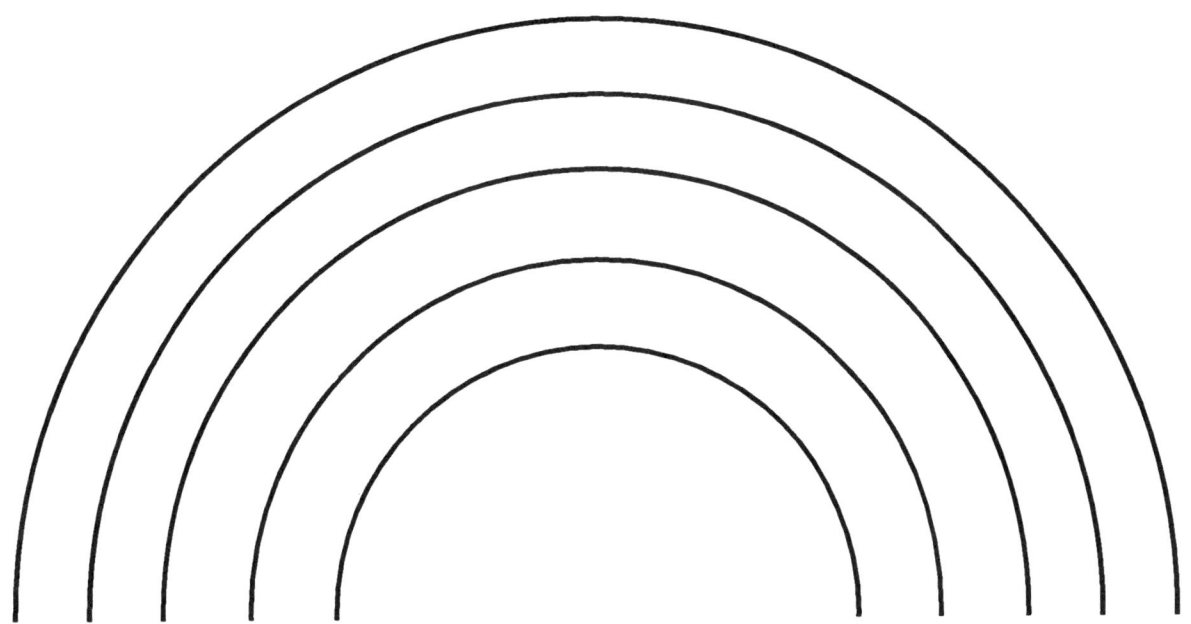

~ 8 ~

I Go to Church as Part of God's Family

Theme: Church

Opening Song: "Church"
      (Tune, "Farmer in the Dell")

> In church I pray to God.
> In church I pray to God.
> I belong to God's family.
> And in church I pray to God.
> In church I hear God's Word.
> In church I hear God's Word.
> God's Word comes from the Bible.
> And in church I hear God's Word.

Greeting: We are here to celebrate going to church as part of God's family.

Reading: "So God blessed the seventh day and made it holy." Genesis 2:3

Response to God's Word

Leader:	We are all part of God's family.
Children:	Thanks be to God.
Leader:	God wants us to gather to worship together in the house of God, the church.
Children:	Thanks be to God.
Leader:	We have a special day to visit God's house; God made that day holy.
Children:	Thanks be to God.
Leader:	This special day is Sunday.
Children:	Thanks be to God.

Prayer object: church *(Give each child a church to color and cut out.)*

Thank You Prayer

Leader:	For giving us your church as a special place to be with you,
Children:	Thank you, God.
Leader:	For giving us Sunday, a holy day,
Children:	Thank you, God.
Leader:	We are happy to visit God in church.
Children:	Thank you, God.
Leader:	*(to children)* Do any of you have something special you are thankful for that you would like to share?
Children:	Thank you, God. *(Use this response after each child's prayer.)*

Closing Song: "Church"

~ *I Go to Church as Part of God's Family* ~

~ 9 ~
Prayer Is Listening and Talking to God

Theme: Prayer

Opening Song: "When I Pray"
(Tune, "Mary Had a Little Lamb")

> When I pray, I listen and talk,
> Listen to God, talk to God;
> When I pray, I listen and talk,
> I listen and talk to God.

Greeting: We are here to celebrate the joy we feel when we pray to God.

Reading: "Ask and you will receive. Seek and you will find." Matthew 7:7

Response to God's Word

Leader:	God is always here for us. All we need do is talk to God and listen to God.
Children:	Thanks be to God.
Leader:	Prayer is talking to God and listening to God.
Children:	Thanks be to God.
Leader:	We feel joyful when we pray to God.
Children:	Thanks be to God.
Leader:	When we pray, we offer God our love.
Children:	Thanks be to God.

Prayer Object: praying hands *(Give each child praying hands to color and cut out.)*

Thank You Prayer

Leader:	For always being there for us to talk to,
Children:	Thank you, God.
Leader:	For the special prayer we learned from Jesus,
Children:	Thank you, God.
Leader:	We will say this special prayer together now:
All:	Our Father, who art in heaven, hallowed be thy name; thy kingdom come; thy will be done, on earth as it is in heaven. Give us this day our daily bread; and forgive us our trespasses as we forgive those who trespass against us; and lead us not into temptation, but deliver us from evil. Amen.
Leader:	*(to children)* Do any of you have something special you are thankful for that you would like to share?
Children:	Thank you, God. *(Use this response after each child's prayer.)*

Closing Song: "When I Pray"

~ *Prayer Is Listening and Talking to God* ~

~ *Prayer Is Listening and Talking to God* ~

~ 10 ~

We Have Much to Be Thankful For

Theme: Thanksgiving

Opening Song: "We Are Thankful"
(Tune, "Are You Sleeping?")

> We are thankful, we are thankful,
> To our Lord, to our Lord,
> For your many blessings,
> For your many blessings,
> Thank you, Lord; thank you, Lord.

Greeting: We are here in honor of the celebration of Thanksgiving.

Reading: "Give thanks to the Lord, for the Lord is good." Psalm 106:1

Response to God's Word
Leader: We remember the first Thanksgiving when Native Americans, the Indians, cared and shared with the Pilgrims.
Children: Thanks be to God.
Leader: The turkey is a symbol of Thanksgiving Day.
Children: Thanks be to God.
Leader: God gives us much to be thankful for.
Children: Thanks be to God.
Leader: We have much to be thankful for.
Children: Thanks be to God.

Prayer Object: turkey *(Give each child a turkey to color and cut out.)*

Thank You Prayer
Leader: For the Indians and the Pilgrims who gave us the first Thanksgiving,
Children: Thank you, God.
Leader: For our many blessings,
Children: Thank you, God.
Leader: *(to children)* Do any of you have something special you are thankful for that you would like to share?
Children: Thank you, God. *(Use this response after each child's prayer.)*

Closing Song: "We Are Thankful"

~ We Have Much to Be Thankful For ~

~ 11 ~

Advent Is a Time of Waiting

Theme: Advent—Week 1

Opening Song: "Christmas Star"
      (Tune, "Twinkle, Twinkle, Little Star")

> Twinkle, twinkle, Christmas star,
> You guided shepherds from afar.
> Let your light shine bright today.
> Let our spirits shine, we pray.
> Twinkle, twinkle, Christmas star,
> Guide us brightly from afar.

Greeting: We are here to celebrate the first week of Advent. We are preparing to celebrate the birthday of Jesus. Jesus is the reason for the Christmas season.

Reading: "Love is patient; love is kind." 1 Corinthians 13:4

Response to God's Word

Leader:	Advent is a time of waiting. We are eagerly waiting for Christmas to come.
Children:	Thanks be to God.
Leader:	We will be patient and let our love shine, just as the stars shine.
Children:	Thanks be to God.
Leader:	We will show kindness to all we meet as we wait for Christmas.
Children:	Thanks be to God.

Prayer Object: star *(Give each child a star to color and cut out.)*

Thank You Prayer

Leader:	For sending us Jesus,
Children:	Thank you, God.
Leader:	For helping us to be patient and kind as we wait for Christmas,
Children:	Thank you, God.
Leader:	*(to children)* Do any of you have something special you are thankful for that you would like to share?
Children:	Thank you, God. *(Use this response after each child's prayer.)*

Closing Song: "Christmas Star"

~ *Advent Is a Time of Waiting—Week 1* ~

~ 12 ~

We Prepare Our Hearts for Christmas

Theme: Advent—Week 2

Opening Song: "We Love Jesus"
        (Tune, "London Bridge")

> We love Jesus, yes we do,
> Yes we do, yes we do.
> We love Jesus, yes we do.
> He came to us on Christmas.

Greeting: We are here in celebration of the second week of Advent. We continue to prepare for the birthday of Jesus.

Reading: "Prepare a way for the Lord." Luke 3:4

Response to God's Word
Leader: God showed great love for us by sending us Jesus.
Children: Thanks be to God.
Leader: We prepare our hearts for Jesus by showing love and kindness toward others.
Children: Thanks be to God.
Leader: We love Jesus.
Children: Thanks be to God.

Prayer Object: heart *(Give each child a heart to color and cut out.)*

Thank You Prayer
Leader: For your great gift of love, Jesus,
Children: Thank you, God.
Leader: We will prepare for Christmas by sharing our love with others.
Children: Thank you, God.
Leader: *(to children)* Do any of you have something special you are thankful for that you would like to share?
Children: Thank you, God. *(Use this response after each child's prayer.)*

Closing Song: "We Love Jesus"

~ We Prepare Our Hearts for Christmas—Week 2 ~

~ 13 ~

Christmas Will Soon Be Here

Theme: Advent—Week 3

Opening Song: "The Angel Brought Good News"
(Tune, "Farmer in the Dell")

> The angel brought good news,
> The angel brought good news,
> Of Jesus' birth on Christmas day.
> The angel brought good news.

Greeting: We are here in celebration of the third week of Advent. Christmas will soon be here and our wait will be over.

Reading: "Clap your hands for joy, all peoples." Psalm 47:1

Response to God's Word
Leader: The angel brought the wonderful news of Jesus' birth.
Children: Thanks be to God.
Leader: This news is cause for great rejoicing and celebrating.
Children: Thanks be to God.
Leader: Christmas is a joyful time.
Children: Thanks be to God.
Leader: We will clap our hands with joy.
Children: Thanks be to God.

Prayer Object: angel *(Give each child an angel to color and cut out.)*

Thank You Prayer
Leader: For sending us the angel who brought the good news,
Children: Thank you, God.
Leader: We will share our joy with others.
Children: Thank you, God.
Leader: *(to children)* Do any of you have something special you are thankful for that you would like to share?
Children: Thank you, God. *(Use this response after each child's prayer.)*

Closing Song: "The Angel Brought Good News"

~ *Christmas Will Soon Be Here—Week 3* ~

~ 14 ~

We Celebrate Jesus' Birthday

Theme: Advent—Week 4

Opening Song: "Happy Birthday to Jesus"

> Happy birthday to you,
> Happy birthday to you,
> Happy birthday, dear Jesus,
> Happy birthday to you.

Greeting: We are here to celebrate the joy of Jesus' birthday which took place a long time ago in Bethlehem.

Reading: "All this happened to fulfill what the Lord had said through the prophet: 'The virgin shall be with child and give birth to a son, and they shall call him Emmanuel; a name which means God is with us.'" Matthew 1:22–23

Response to God's Word
Leader: On that first Christmas eve, Mary and Joseph traveled to Bethlehem and stayed in a stable because there was no room for them in the inn. There Jesus was born and Mary placed him in a manger.
Children: Thanks be to God.
Leader: Jesus, the light of the world, has come into our lives.
Children: Thanks be to God.
Leader: We rejoice because God is with us.
Children: Thanks be to God.

Prayer Object: candle *(Give each child a candle to color and cut out.)*

Thank You Prayer
Leader: For the joy and happiness that Jesus' birthday brings,
Children: Thank you, God.
Leader: We want to share Jesus' light with everyone we know.
Children: Thank you, God.
Leader: *(to children)* Do any of you have something special you are thankful for that you would like to share?
Children: Thank you, God. *(Use this response after each child's prayer.)*

Closing Song: "Happy Birthday to Jesus"

~ We Celebrate Jesus' Birthday—Week 4 ~

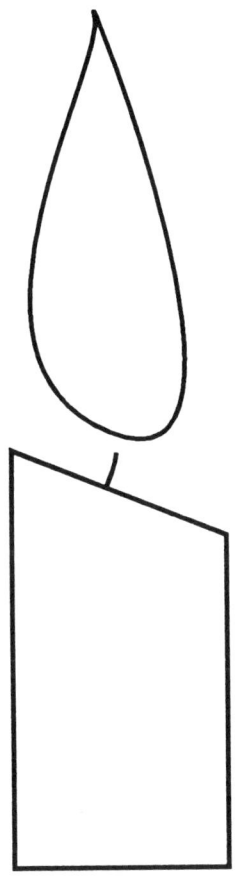

~ 15 ~

We Experience God's World with Our Five Senses

Theme: Five Senses

Opening Song: "God Gave Me"
  (Tune, "London Bridge")

> God gave me my eyes to see,
> Ears to hear, nose to smell.
> God gave me my mouth to taste,
> And my hands to touch.

Greeting: We are here to thank God for our gifts of seeing, hearing, smelling, tasting, and touching.

Reading: "God has wonderfully made us." Psalm 139:13–14

Response to God's Word

Leader:	God has given us many gifts to use to learn about our world.
Children:	Thanks be to God.
Leader:	God created us with love in a wonderful way.
Children:	Thanks be to God.
Leader:	God has given us eyes to see and ears to hear.
Children:	Thanks be to God.
Leader:	God has given us mouths to taste, noses to smell, and hands to touch.
Children:	Thanks be to God.

Prayer Object: face *(Give each child a face to color and cut out.)*

Thank You Prayer

Leader:	For your gift of our five senses,
Children:	Thank you, God.
Leader:	For making us in a wonderful way,
Children:	Thank you, God.
Leader:	We will use our gifts to learn more about your wonderful world.
Children:	Thank you, God.
Leader:	*(to children)* Do any of you have something special you are thankful for that you would like to share?
Children:	Thank you, God. *(Use this response after each child's prayer.)*

Closing Song: "God Gave Me"

~ *We Experience God's World with Our Five Senses* ~

~ 16 ~

We Can Help Others

Theme: Being a Helper

Opening Song: "A Helper"
  (Tune, "Mary Had a Little Lamb")

> Jesus showed us how to help,
> By being kind, showing love.
> Jesus showed us how to help,
> I'll be a helper too.

Greeting: We are here to celebrate helpfulness as a way to show kindness and love for others.

Reading: "Love God with all your heart and your neighbor as yourself." Luke 10:27

Response to God's Word
Leader: Jesus helped people who were sick.
Children: Thanks be to God.
Leader: Jesus helped people who could not walk.
Children: Thanks be to God.
Leader: Jesus helped people who could not see.
Children: Thanks be to God.
Leader: Jesus loves little children. He wants them to use their helping hands to reach out to others.
Children: Thanks be to God.

Prayer Object: hand *(Give each child a hand to color and cut out.)*

Thank You Prayer
Leader: For showing us how to help others,
Children: Thank you, God.
Leader: We will show kindness and love for others by being helpful.
Children: Thank you, God.
Leader: (to children) Do any of you have something special you are thankful for that you would like to share?
Children: Thank you, God. *(Use this response after each child's prayer.)*

Closing Song: "A Helper"

~ *We Can Help Others* ~

~ 17 ~
We Can Share With Others

Theme: Sharing

Opening Song: "Share with Friends"
(Tune, "Did You Ever See a Lassie?")

> The more we learn to share with friends,
> To share with friends, to share with friends,
> The more we learn to share with friends,
> The happier we'll be.

Greeting: Today we celebrate the joy of sharing. Sharing is a way we show love and concern for others.

Reading: "I was hungry and you gave me food. I was thirsty and you gave me drink." Matthew 25:35

Response to God's Word
Leader: Jesus always shared with people because he loved them.
Children: Thanks be to God.
Leader: Jesus shared his food, shelter—all he had to give.
Children: Thanks be to God.
Leader: We can be like Jesus by sharing with our friends.
Children: Thanks be to God.
Leader: We can share our love of Jesus with our friends.
Children: Thanks be to God.

Prayer Object: balloon (*Give each child a balloon to color and cut out.*)

Thank You Prayer
Leader: For sending us Jesus to show us how to share,
Children: Thank you, God.
Leader: We will share with our friends. We can share toys, balloons, snacks, and love.
Children: Thank you, God.
Leader: (*to children*) Do any of you have something special you are thankful for that you would like to share?
Children: Thank you, God. (*Use this response after each child's prayer.*)

Closing Song: "Share with Friends"

~We Can Share With Others~

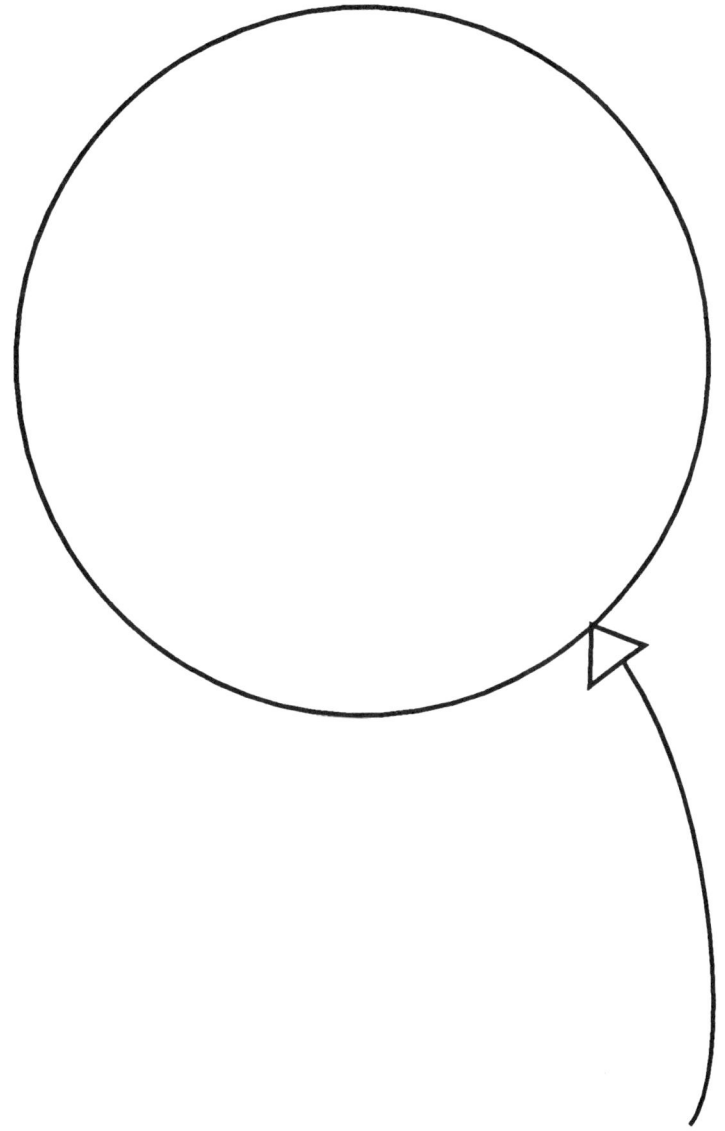

~ 18 ~
Jesus Is My Special Friend

Theme: My Special Friend, Jesus

Opening Song: "Jesus Is My Special Friend"
(Tune, "London Bridge")

> Jesus is my special friend,
> Special friend, special friend.
> Jesus is my special friend,
> I love him very much.

Greeting: We are here in honor of our special friend, Jesus.

Reading: "Treat others the way you would have them treat you." Matthew 7:12

Response to God's Word
Leader: Jesus is our special friend who loves us very much.
Children: Thanks be to God.
Leader: Jesus forgives us when we make a mistake.
Children: Thanks be to God.
Leader: Jesus wants us to live by this golden rule—treat others the way we wish to be treated.
Children: Thanks be to God.
Leader: Jesus will never stop being our special friend.
Children: Thanks be to God.

Prayer Object: golden heart *(Give each child a heart to color gold and cut out.)*

Thank You Prayer
Leader: For being my special friend,
Children: Thank you, God.
Leader: We will try to live by the golden rule.
Children: Thank you, God.
Leader: *(to children)* Do any of you have something special you are thankful for that you would like to share?
Children: Thank you, God. *(Use this response after each child's prayer.)*

Closing Song: "Jesus Is My Special Friend"

~ *Jesus Is My Special Friend* ~

~ 19 ~

God Understands My Feelings

Theme: Feelings

Opening Song: "Feelings"
    (Tune, "If You're Happy and You Know It")

> If you're happy and you know it, make a smile.
> If you're sad and you know it, make a frown.
> If you're angry and you know it,
> Stamp your feet and really show it.
> If you're happy, sad, or angry, show me now.

Greeting: We all have times when we feel happy, sad, or angry. It is good to know that God always loves us, no matter how we feel.

Reading: "Happy are they who trust in the Lord." Proverbs 16:20

Response to God's Word
Leader:	God has given us much to be happy about.
Children:	Thanks be to God.
Leader:	When we feel sad, Jesus is there to understand. Jesus gives us his love.
Children:	Thanks be to God.
Leader:	We can give our angry feelings to Jesus. Jesus will help us feel better.
Children:	Thanks be to God.
Leader:	If we know Jesus and we trust him, our times of happiness will be great.
Children:	Thanks be to God.

Prayer Object: smile face *(Give each child a smile face to color and cut out.)*

Thank You Prayer
Leader:	For giving us many different feelings,
Children:	Thank you, God.
Leader:	For being with us when feel sad or angry,
Children:	Thank you, God.
Leader:	*(to children)* Do any of you have something special you are thankful for that you would like to share?
Children:	Thank you, God. *(Use this response after each child's prayer.)*

Closing Song: "Feelings"

~ God Understands My Feelings ~

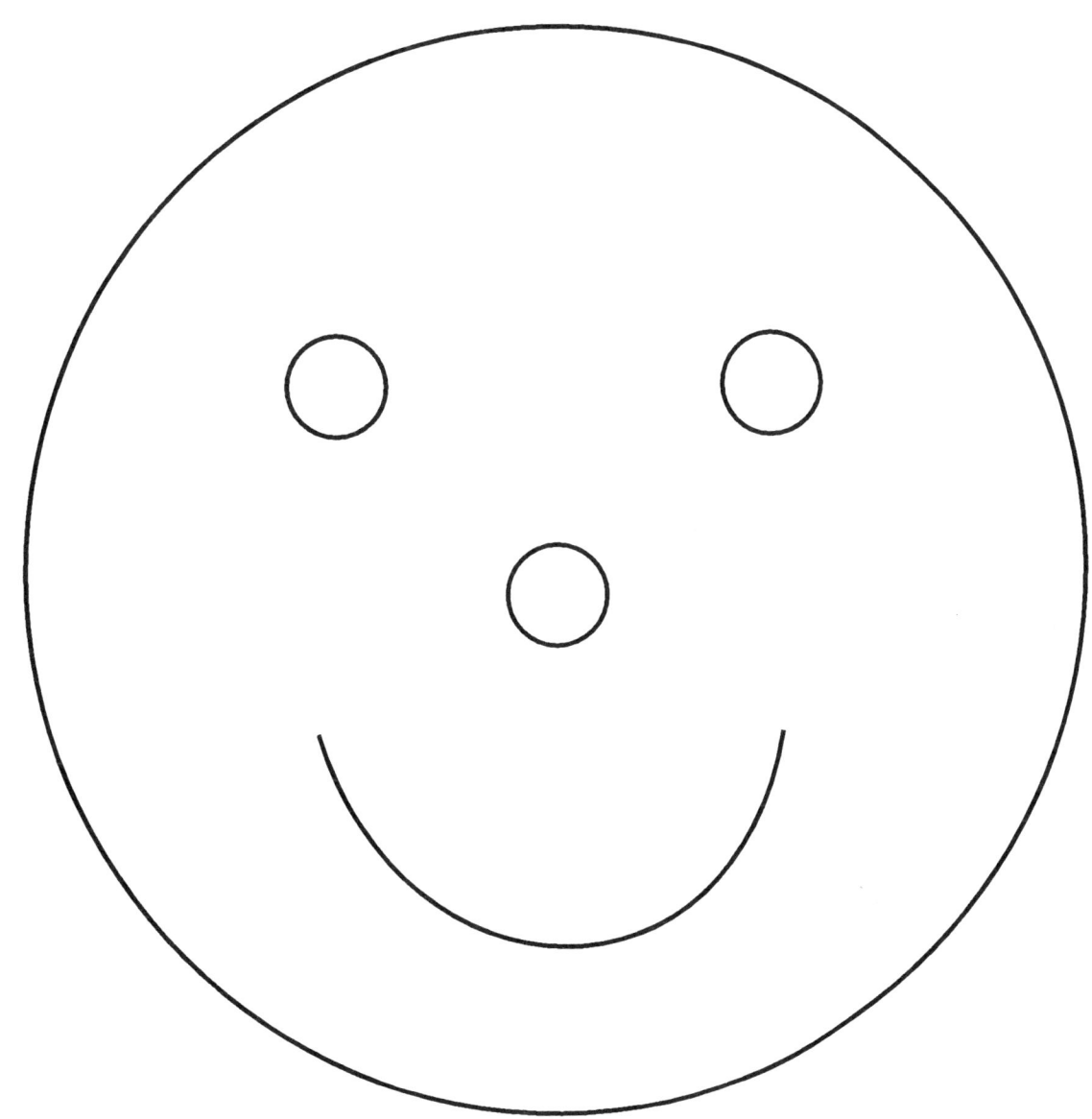

~ 20 ~

God Is With Me When I'm Afraid

Theme: Being Afraid

Opening Song: "Sometimes I Feel Afraid"
(Tune, "Farmer in the Dell")

> Sometimes I feel afraid,
> Sometimes I feel afraid,
> But God is always here with me,
> I need not feel afraid.

Greeting: We are here to celebrate the fact that God is with us even when we are afraid.

Reading: "Fear not, for I am with you." Isaiah 41:10

Response to God's Word
Leader:	We are all afraid sometimes. God knows this. God tells us not to be afraid.
Children:	Thanks be to God.
Leader:	God is always with us.
Children:	Thanks be to God.
Leader:	Sometimes we are afraid of the dark. Remember, God made the light and light always comes after the darkness.
Children:	Thanks be to God.
Leader:	God put the sun in the sky to shine for us in the day.
Children:	Thanks be to God.
Leader:	God put the moon and the stars in the sky to shine for us at night.
Children:	Thanks be to God.

Prayer Object: moon *(Give each child a moon to color and cut out.)*

Thank You Prayer
Leader:	For being with us when we are afraid,
Children:	Thank you, God.
Leader:	For always keeping us in your care,
Children:	Thank you, God.
Leader:	*(to children)* Do any of you have something special you are thankful for that you would like to share?
Children:	Thank you, God. *(Use this response after each child's prayer.)*

Closing Song: "Sometimes I Feel Afraid"

~ *God Is With Me When I'm Afraid* ~

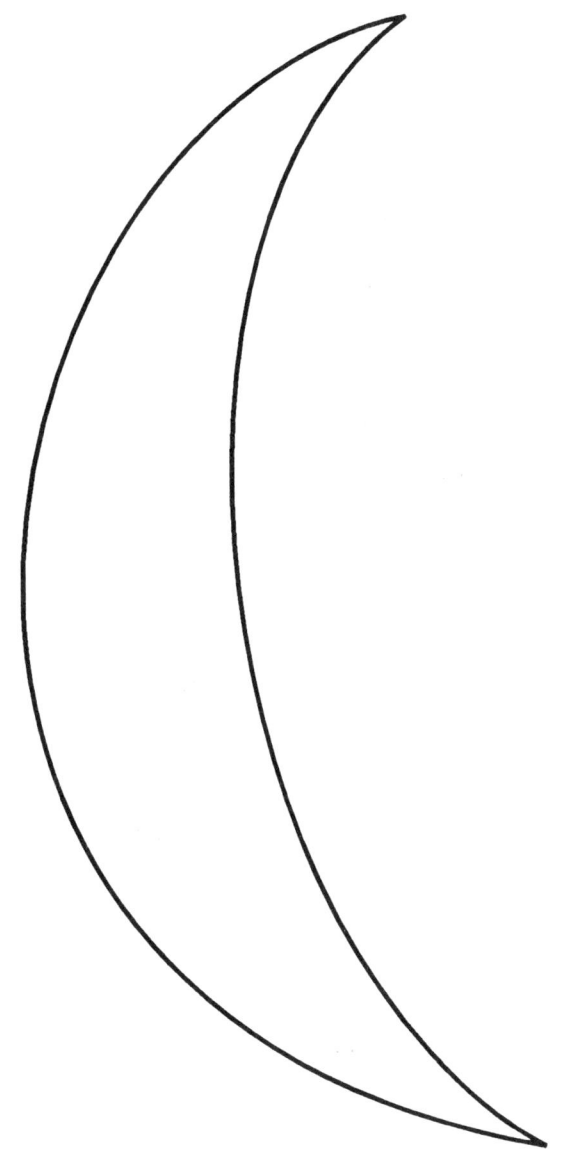

~ *God Is With Me When I'm Afraid* ~

~ 21 ~

We Celebrate Easter

Theme: Easter

Opening Song: "Spring Brings New Life"
(Tune, "Are You Sleeping?")

> Spring brings new life, spring brings new life,
> Winter's gone, winter's gone.
> Easter Sunday's coming, Easter Sunday's coming,
> Thank you, God; thank you, God.

Greeting: We are here to celebrate the coming of Easter.

Reading: "The Lord, your God, is in your midst; God will rejoice over you with gladness; God will renew you in love." Zephaniah 3:17

Response to God's Word

Leader:	God is always with us.
Children:	Thanks be to God.
Leader:	God will always love us.
Children:	Thanks be to God.
Leader:	In the spring, God renews us with many signs of love. For example, the caterpillar "dies" in the cocoon only to emerge from its "tomb" with a beautiful new body as a butterfly.
Children:	Thanks be to God.
Leader:	We rejoice with the gladness that Easter brings.
Children:	Thanks be to God.

Prayer Object: butterfly *(Give each child a butterfly to color and cut out.)*

Thank You Prayer

Leader:	For Jesus,
Children:	Thank you, God.
Leader:	For Easter,
Children:	Thank you, God.
Leader:	For new life in spring,
Children:	Thank you, God.
Leader:	*(to children)* Do any of you have something special you are thankful for that you would like to share?
Children:	Thank you, God. *(Use this response after each child's prayer.)*

Closing Song: "Spring Brings New Life"

~ *We Celebrate Easter* ~

~ 22 ~

Mary Is Our Mother in Heaven

Theme: Mary, Our Heavenly Mother

Opening Song: "Mary's Lamb"
(Tune, "Mary Had a Little Lamb")

> Mary had a little lamb,
> Little lamb, little lamb,
> Mary had a little lamb,
> That little lamb is Jesus.
>
> Now Jesus has a little lamb,
> Little lamb, little lamb.
> Now Jesus has a little lamb,
> That little lamb is you.

Greeting: We are here to celebrate our love for Mary, the mother of Jesus.

Reading: "Love is patient, love is kind." 1 Corinthians 13:14

Response to God's Word
Leader:	God made mothers very special.
Children:	Thanks be to God.
Leader:	Our mothers are patient, kind, and loving.
Children:	Thanks be to God.
Leader:	We love our mothers very much.
Children:	Thanks be to God.
Leader:	We will show love with patience and kindness.
Children:	Thanks be to God.

Prayer Object: mother and child *(Give each child a mother and child to color and cut out.)*

Thank You Prayer
Leader:	For Mary, the mother of Jesus,
Children:	Thank you, God.
Leader:	For our mothers,
Children:	Thank you, God.
Leader:	For our special prayer to Mary,
Children:	Thank you, God.
Leader:	We will say this special prayer together now:
All:	Hail Mary, full of grace! The Lord is with you; blessed are you among women

	and blessed is the fruit of your womb, Jesus. Holy Mary, mother of God, pray for us sinners, now and at the hour of our death. Amen.
Leader:	*(to children)* Do any of you have something special you are thankful for that you would like to share?
Children:	Thank you, God. *(Use this response after each child's prayer.)*

Closing Song: "Mary's Lamb"

~ Mary Is Our Mother in Heaven ~

~ 23 ~

I Am Growing in God's World

Theme: Growing

Opening Song: "Growing"
        (Tune, "London Bridge")

> I am growing, yes I am,
> Yes I am, yes I am.
> I am growing, yes I am,
> And I know God loves me.

Greeting: We are here to celebrate how good it is to be growing up in God's world.

Reading: "Let the little children come to me." Luke 18:16

Response to God's Word
Leader:	We are growing. Each day we get bigger.
Children:	Thanks be to God.
Leader:	Each day our love for Jesus grows stronger.
Children:	Thanks be to God.
Leader:	We know Jesus loves little children. The Bible tells us that he asked for little children to come to him.
Children:	Thanks be to God.
Leader:	We have come to Jesus.
Children:	Thanks be to God.
Leader:	It feels good to be growing in God's world.
Children:	Thanks be to God.

Prayer Object: balloon (*Give each child a balloon to color and cut out.*)

Thank You Prayer
Leader:	For helping me to grow,
Children:	Thank you, God.
Leader:	For your love of little children,
Children:	Thank you, God.
Leader:	(*to children*) Do any of you have something special you are thankful for that you would like to share?
Children:	Thank you, God. (*Use this response after each child's prayer.*)

Closing Song: "Growing"

~ *I Am Growing in God's World* ~

~ 24 ~

St. Valentine Loves Little Children

Theme: St. Valentine—February 14

Opening Song: "St. Valentine"
(Tune, "I'm a Little Teapot")

St. Valentine loved children very much,
He sent them cards to show them he cared.
And now we remember his love so true,
By having valentines to give and candy hearts to share.

Greeting: We are having a special celebration in honor of St. Valentine.

Reading: "Love one another as I have loved you." John 15:17

Response to God's Word
Leader: Long ago children would come to sing and play in the church garden of a gentle priest named Valentine. One day a cruel king put Valentine in prison. St. Valentine did not forget the children he loved so much. He sent them letters and told them it was alright to continue to play in his garden while he was away.
Children: Thanks be to God.
Leader: We remember St. Valentine by sending cards full of love like the ones he sent.
Children: Thanks be to God.
Leader: We will remember to love one another as God has loved us.
Children: Thanks be to God.

Prayer Object: heart (*Give each child a heart to color red and cut out.*)

Thank You Prayer
Leader: For sending us the gentle kindness of St. Valentine,
Children: Thank you, God.
Leader: We will show love for our friends and family by sending valentines.
Children: Thank you, God.
Leader: (*to children*) Do any of you have something special you are thankful for that you would like to share?
Children: Thank you, God. (*Use this response after each child's prayer.*)

Closing Song: "St. Valentine"

~ St. Valentine Loves Little Children ~

~ 25 ~

We Celebrate Mary's Birthday

Theme: Birthday of Mary—September 8

Opening Song: "Happy Birthday to Mary"

> Happy birthday to Mary,
> Happy birthday to Mary,
> Happy birthday, dear Mary,
> Happy birthday to you.

Greeting: We are here to celebrate the birthday of Mary, the mother of Jesus.

Reading: "How wonderfully God shows love for me." based on Psalm 89:28

Response to God's Word
Leader: Mary was very good. She loved God.
Children: Thanks be to God.
Leader: She obeyed her mother and father.
Children: Thanks be to God.
Leader: God loves Mary and because she was so good, God chose her to be the mother of Jesus.
Children: Thanks be to God.
Leader: Mary is our mother, too. She is our heavenly mother.
Children: Thanks be to God.

Prayer Object: birthday cake *(Give each child a cake to color and cut out.)*

Thank You Prayer
Leader: For Mary,
Children: Thank you, God.
Leader: For our special prayer for Mary,
Children: Thank you, God.
Leader: Let us pray this special prayer together now:
All: Hail Mary, full of grace! The Lord is with you; blessed are you among women, and blessed is the fruit of your womb, Jesus. Holy Mary, mother of God, pray for us sinners, now and at the hour of our death. Amen.
Leader: *(to children)* Do any of you have something special you are thankful for that you would like to share?
Children: Thank you, God. *(Use this response after each child's prayer.)*

Closing Song: "May the Dear Lord Bless You"
(Tune, "Happy Birthday")

May the dear Lord bless you,
May the dear Lord bless you,
May the dear Lord bless Mary,
May the dear Lord bless you.

~ We Celebrate Mary's Birthday ~

~ 26 ~

St. Thérèse Was the Little Flower of Jesus

Theme: Feast of St. Thérèse—October 1

Opening Song: "Little Flower"
 (Tune, "Farmer in the Dell")

> God fills our world with flowers,
> God fills our world with flowers,
> Roses, daisies, violets, too,
> God fills our world with flowers.

Greeting: We are here to celebrate the feast of St. Thérèse, the Little Flower of Jesus.

Reading: "The earth is filled with your blessings." Psalm 104:13

Response to God's Word
Leader: St. Thérèse loved the flowers God made. She knew that even though some flowers may seem more beautiful than others, God lets the rain fall and the sun shine on all of them. She called herself the "little flower of Jesus."
Children: Thanks be to God.
Leader: St. Thérèse knew that although God made people different, God loves all of them.
Children: Thanks be to God.
Leader: It does not matter how big or small, or what color their skin may be; God loves all people.
Children: Thanks be to God.

Prayer Object: rose *(Give each child a rose to color and cut out.)*

Thank You Prayer
Leader: For the beautiful flowers that brighten our world,
Children: Thank you, God.
Leader: For St. Thérèse, who showed us how special your care is,
Children: Thank you, God.
Leader: *(to children)* Do any of you have something special you are thankful for that you would like to share?
Children: Thank you, God. *(Use this response after each child's prayer.)*

Closing Song: "Little Flower"

~ St. Thérèse Was the Little Flower of Jesus ~

~ 27 ~

I Have a Guardian Angel

Theme: Feast of the Guardian Angels—October 2

Opening Song: "Guardian Angels"
(Tune, "Mary Had a Little Lamb")

> Guardian angels protect us,
> Protect us, protect us.
> Guardian angels protect us,
> They are with us all the time.

Greeting: We are here to celebrate the feast of the guardian angels, the special messengers from God.

Reading: "I am sending an angel before you, to guard you on your way." Exodus 23:20

Response to God's Word

Leader:	God has given each of us a guardian angel to care for us.
Children:	Thanks be to God.
Leader:	God has given each of us a guardian angel to help us to love.
Children:	Thanks be to God.
Leader:	Our guardian angels are always nearby to protect us from harm.
Children:	Thanks be to God.
Leader:	Our guardian angels are special messengers from God.
Children:	Thanks be to God.

Prayer Object: angel *(Give each child an angel to color and cut out.)*

Thank You Prayer

Leader:	For our guardian angels who are our special friends,
Children:	Thank you, God.
Leader:	We pray their special prayer:
All:	Angel of God, my guardian dear,
	To whom God's love commits me here,
	Ever this day be at my side,
	To light, to guard, to rule and guide. Amen.
Leader:	*(to children)* Do any of you have something special you are thankful for that you would like to share?
Children:	Thank you, God. *(Use this response after each child's prayer.)*

Closing Song: "Guardian Angels"

~ I Have a Guardian Angel ~

~ 28 ~

St. Francis Loved God's Creatures

Theme: Feast of St. Francis—October 4

Opening Song: "God's Creatures"
        (Tune, "Row, Row, Row Your Boat")

> Fish, birds, bears, and bees,
> God has made them all.
> Our world is full of the creatures God made.
> St. Francis loved them all.

Greeting: We are here to celebrate the feast of St. Francis and his love for all of God's creatures.

Reading: "Lord, you have made so many things! How wisely you made them all! Earth is filled with your creatures." Psalm 104:24

Response to God's Word
Leader:	Francis is a saint in heaven with God.
Children:	Thanks be to God.
Leader:	He loved God's creatures. He called God's creatures his sisters and brothers.
Children:	Thanks be to God.
Leader:	He helps us to know that all of God's creatures are good.
Children:	Thanks be to God.
Leader:	We will take care of God's creatures.
Children:	Thanks be to God.

Prayer Object: bird *(Give each child a bird to color and cut out.)*

Thank You Prayer
Leader:	For filling our world with your wonderful creatures,
Children:	Thank you, God.
Leader:	For sending us St. Francis, who taught us how to love your creatures,
Children:	Thank you, God.
Leader:	We want to be kind to all that you have created.
Children:	Thank you, God.
Leader:	*(to children)* Do any of you have something special you are thankful for that you would like to share?
Children:	Thank you, God. *(Use this response after each child's prayer.)*

Closing Song: "God's Creatures"

~ *St. Francis Loved God's Creatures* ~

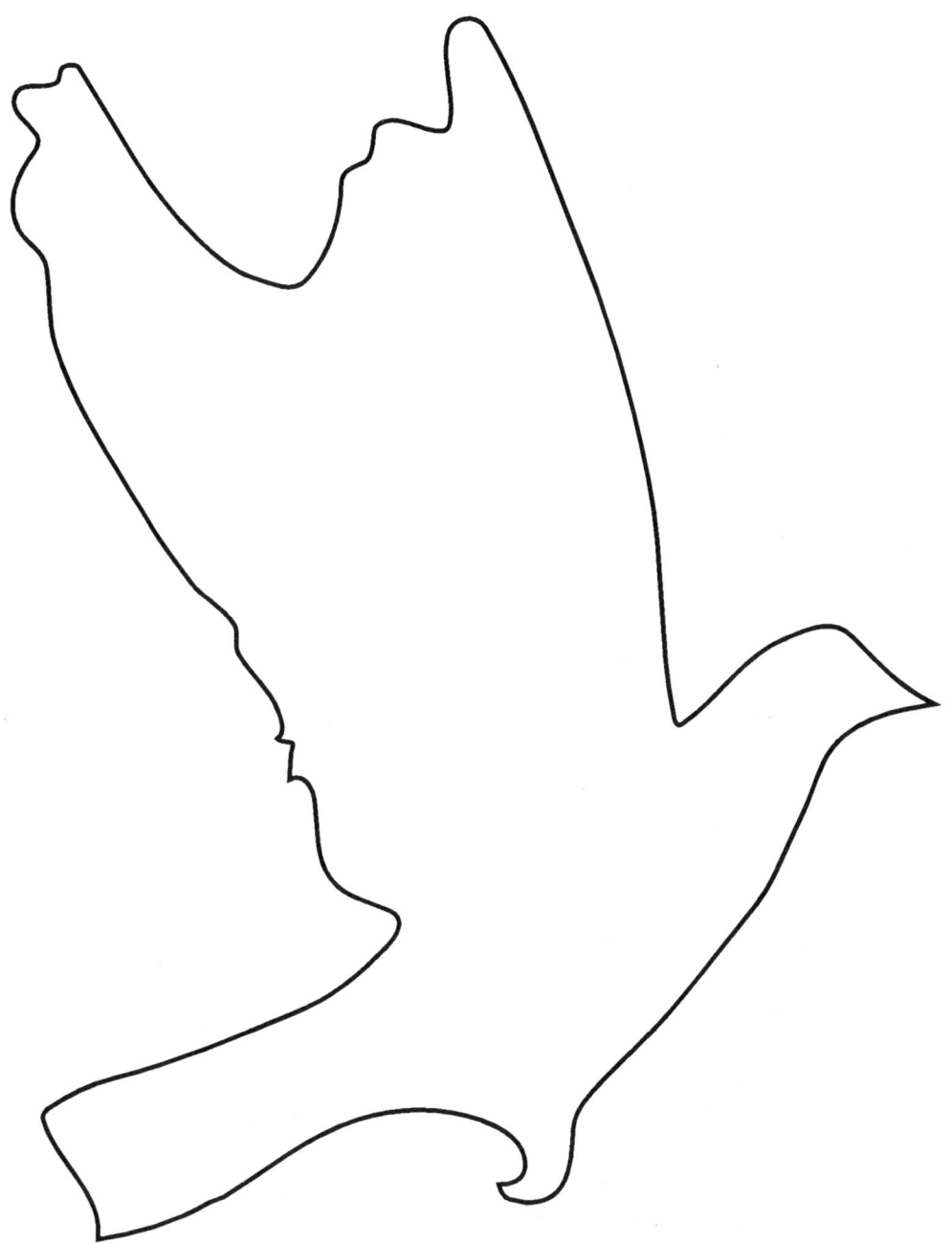

~ 29 ~

St. Patrick Told Us of God's Love

Theme: Feast of St. Patrick—March 17

Opening Song: "The Green Shamrock"
(Tune, "Farmer in the Dell")

> God gave us the green shamrock,
> God gave us the green shamrock.
> The Father, Son, and Spirit are one.
> God gave us the green shamrock.

Greeting: We celebrate today in honor of St. Patrick.

Reading: "I am in the Father and the Father is in me...and the Holy Spirit will instruct you in everything." John 14:11,26

Response to God's Word
Leader: St. Patrick was a priest who brought the faith to Ireland.
Children: Thanks be to God.
Leader: He found Ireland to be a beautiful country and the shamrock a beautiful symbol of the sign of the Father, Son, and Holy Spirit.
Children: Thanks be to God.
Leader: We will remember St. Patrick and the beautiful shamrock when we make the sign of the cross.
Children: Thanks be to God.

Prayer Object: shamrock *(Give each child a shamrock to color and cut out.)*

Thank You Prayer
Leader: For St. Patrick,
Children: Thank you, God.
Leader: God the Father, God the Son, God the Holy Spirit, you are one.
Children: Thank you, God.
Leader: *(to children)* Do any of you have something special you are thankful for that you would like to share?
Children: Thank you, God. *(Use this response after each child's prayer.)*

Closing Song: "The Green Shamrock"

~ St. Patrick Told Us of God's Love ~

~ 30 ~

St. Joseph Was a Loving Father

Theme: St. Joseph—March 19

Opening Song: "St. Joseph Was a Carpenter"
(Tune, "This is the Way")

> St. Joseph was a carpenter,
> A carpenter, a carpenter.
> St. Joseph was a carpenter,
> And Jesus was his helper.

Greeting: We are here to celebrate the feast of St. Joseph, the loving foster father of Jesus.

Reading: "Joseph was a righteous man." Matthew 1:19

Response to God's Word
Leader:	Joseph was a loving husband and foster father.
Children:	Thanks be to God.
Leader:	Joseph loved and trusted God.
Children:	Thanks be to God.
Leader:	Joseph was a carpenter. He enjoyed having Jesus help him in his workshop.
Children:	Thanks be to God.
Leader:	Joseph followed the golden rule: he always treated others the way he wished to be treated.
Children:	Thanks be to God.

Prayer Object: hammer and saw (*Give each child a hammer and saw to color and cut out.*)

Thank You Prayer
Leader:	For sending us St. Joseph,
Children:	Thank you, God.
Leader:	St. Joseph was a good man. He prayed to God and took good care of his family.
Children:	Thank you, God.
Leader:	(*to children*) Do any of you have something special you are thankful for that you would like to share?
Children:	Thank you, God. (*Use this response after each child's prayer.*)

Closing Song: "St. Joseph Was a Carpenter"

~ *St. Joseph Was a Loving Father* ~

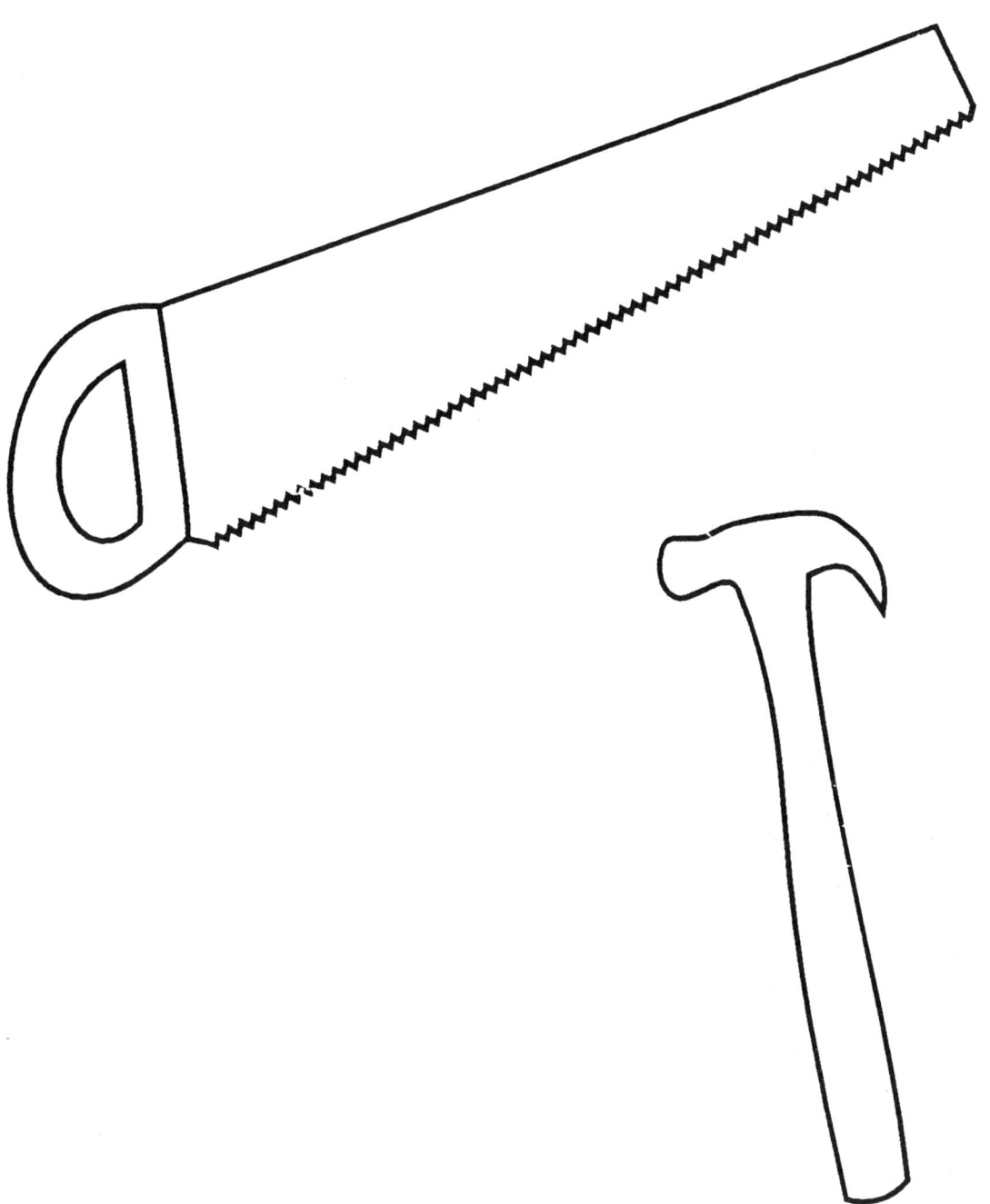

Of Related Interest...

Praying with Children
Gwen Costello

28 prayer services for a variety of situations. Covers the seasons of the year, liturgical feasts and special occasions. For teachers, catechists and parents.
ISBN: 0-89622-439-2, 96 pp, $9.95

Dear Jesus, Dear Child
Guided Meditations for Young Children
Deborah Roslak and Linda Orber

Joys, fears and needs of primary-grade children are focused on here in a format that includes letters written to Jesus by children, examples of how Jesus might respond and teacher-led guided meditations.
ISBN: 0-89622-508-9, 96 pp, $9.95

Children, Imagination and Prayer
Creative Techniques for Middle Grade Students
Pat Egan Dexter

Encourages the use of imagination in teaching children how to pray. Offers a creative guided imagery technique that allows children to explore their thoughts and feelings.
ISBN: 0-89622-565-8, 80 pp, $7.95

Leading Students to Prayer
Ideas and Suggestions from A to Z
Kathleen Glavich

A practical, hands-on guide. Using an alphabet-based approach to introduce various elements to prayer, it focuses on ways to help students build a loving relationship with God. Adaptable for primary grades through high school.
ISBN: 0-89622-549-6, 160 pp, $12.95

Seasonal Prayer Services for Teenagers
Greg Dues

16 prayer services that help teenagers understand the themes found in the holidays of the seasons, the church year and the civic year.
ISBN: 0-89622-473-2, $9.95

Teen Prayer Services
20 Themes for Reflection
Kevin Regan

Helps teens touch life by inviting them into dialogue with God. Services focus on issues important to teens. Great for retreats, special sessions and regular classes.
ISBN: 0-89622-520-8, 80 pp, $9.95

Available at religious bookstores or from

TWENTY-THIRD PUBLICATIONS
P.O. Box 180
Mystic, CT 06355
1-800-321-0411